SAMSUNG GALAXY FEATURES AND WHAT TO EXPECT 2024

Addressing Community Concerns and Embracing Innovation

Masha Paid

Table of Contents

Introductio...5

Creating the Conditions for Innovation.................... 8

Chapter 1.. 12

Overview of Announcements.............................. 12

Unveiling the Latest from Samsung........................15

Chapter 2.. 19

Device Highlights.. 19

• Decoding the Galaxy S24 Series........................22

• Galaxy Ring Teaser:.. 25

Chapter 3.. 30

Software Updates.. 30

Elevating User Experience through Software.........34

Chapter 4.. 39

Trade-In Programs and Pricing.............................. 39

Navigating the Galaxy Trade-Ins and Pricing
Strategy... 41

Echoes from r/samsung: User Sentiments Unveiled..
50

Chapter 6.. 55

Challenges and Concerns.................................... 55

Addressing Community Concerns........................ 57

Chapter 7.. 61

Future Expectations.. 61

What's Ahead for Unpacked 2024........................ 65

Conclusion... 70

The Impact of Unpacked 2024............................72

Introductio

In the context of CES 2024, Samsung's Unpacked event was a spectacular spectacle that drew tech aficionados and industry insiders with the sparkling lights of Las Vegas. It was a demonstration of technological innovation, a window into the future of technology, and a sign of an artificial intelligence-driven networked world. The air was electric with anticipation as Samsung's 'AI for All' pavilion opened, a collective breath held by those anxious to see the tech giant reveal its newest innovations.

Samsung's exhibit, located in the center of CES, mirrored the theme of "AI for All: Connectivity in the Age of AI." A concept that pledged not just innovation but also a dedication to enhancing lives in every way, from the cosy confines of our homes to the exciting environments of the workplace and all points in between. The setting was set for a study of how artificial intelligence may transform human experiences if it were to be smoothly incorporated into our everyday lives.

The air was heavy with the awareness of environmental duty as guests entered Samsung's Sustainability Zone. The exhibit demonstrated not just state-of-the-art technology but also a dedication to environmentally sensitive ideas. Recycled material walls served as a symbol of Samsung's commitment to environmental sustainability. Through the circular workshop, information on Samsung's resource circularity initiatives, accessibility improvements, and environmental strategy was revealed.

The tour continued smoothly from sustainability to the SmartThings Zone, an interactive area where guests could explore Samsung's constantly developing home environment. The area, which included 196 SmartThings-compatible gadgets and goods from 48 partner businesses, was evidence of Samsung's goal of fostering better living. Guests explored scenarios that portrayed various rooms and chores in a house, imagining how SmartThings may improve and simplify their everyday life.

The Screen Experience Zone redefined entertainment with its captivating demonstration of how AI technology improves Samsung's screens. Watching video on premium TVs—like the recently released Transparent MICRO LED—has become an immersive experience. The zone aimed to redefine how you experience visual material, not simply what you see. The updated Ballie, Samsung's AI companion robot, was shown to the attendees with the promise of more personalised services.

The tour proceeded into the Home Experience Zone, where the emphasis was on the ways AI technology reduces the inconvenience of everyday activities and duties. Samsung's line of Bespoke home appliances, which includes the AI Laundry ComboTM and the 4-Door FlexTM Refrigerator with AI Family HubTM+, are transforming laundry management and food component handling with their intelligent capabilities like AI OptiWashTM and AI Vision Inside.

The Mobile Experience Zone, an area devoted to Samsung's mobile devices, was where the big show took place. Here, participants may try out the enhanced AI features, feel the strength of the newest Galaxy Book4 series, and examine its precise touchscreen. The area served as an example of Samsung's collaborations with leading companies in the market, including Microsoft, to create a more interconnected Galaxy environment.

In addition to seeing the reveal of technical wonders, CES 2024 offered a glimpse into Samsung's fundamental principles, which include sustainability, connection, and an unwavering commitment to improving user experiences. This piece attempts to examine the nuances, investigate community responses, and analyse the technological specifics that characterise Samsung's future trajectory as we go into the core of Unpacked 2024. Come along on this fascinating journey across the fields of innovation and AI, where each discovery marks a step toward a society that is smarter and more interconnected.

Creating the Conditions for Innovation

Innovation is the driving force behind industry advancement in the rapidly changing field of technology, revolutionising our daily lives, careers, and social interactions. Creating the conditions for innovation is a multifaceted process that combines strategic planning, imaginative thinking, and the unwavering search for answers to the problems that characterise our day.

Understanding the complexities of the environment that innovation travels through is crucial before diving headfirst into it. Not only have cutting-edge technologies, the internet of things, and artificial intelligence rapidly progressed, but they have also blurred the barriers between the digital and physical worlds, redefining what is possible. The constant speed of change highlights the need for both people and organisations to adapt, spurring the search for ground-breaking concepts and creative solutions.

In order to create an environment conducive to innovation, leadership is essential. Change is architected by visionaries who can go forward into unexplored territory, accepting uncertainty and seizing opportunity. A recurring theme in the biographies of prosperous executives is their capacity to create an environment that encourages innovation, taking calculated risks, and an unwavering focus on quality.

Creative settings are conducive to innovation. Businesses that put money into developing an innovation environment encourage teamwork, candid dialogue, and interdisciplinary thinking. The capacity to foster an environment where many viewpoints are valued, failure is seen as a necessary step toward success, and experimentation is encouraged may spark ground-breaking inventions in both start-ups and well-established businesses.

With the fourth industrial revolution just around the corner, technology is becoming a vital tool for fostering creativity. Technological developments provide visionaries the means to transform ideas into reality, from advances in quantum computing to the incorporation of artificial intelligence into daily life. Comprehending the convergence of technology and innovation becomes crucial for those who want to influence the future.

Innovation is not limited by geography in a globalised society. Global partnerships generate a rich tapestry of viewpoints and ideas by bringing together brains from different backgrounds. Global knowledge sharing and resource sharing increase the likelihood of ground-breaking inventions that tackle global issues like health care inequalities and climate change.

Ethical concerns become the compass that directs innovation as we open up new horizons. Consideration must be given to issues pertaining to data privacy, ethical AI use, and the effects of developing technologies on society. In order to foster innovation, one must be dedicated to moral behaviour that guarantees the just and responsible distribution of the advantages of advancement.

Innovation travels are seldom without difficulties. The innovation frontier is dotted with both failures and successes, from negotiating regulatory environments to overcoming opposition to change. Examining case studies of businesses that have adopted innovation effectively may provide important insights into the tactics that result in revolutionary transformation and long-term expansion.

Looking to the future is essential for laying the groundwork for innovation. By predicting the trends that will reshape the world in the future, we may put ourselves at the forefront of advancement. The possibilities are endless, ranging from the promise of bioengineering to the incorporation of augmented reality into daily life. Those with the courage to dream will be the ones creating the breakthroughs that will shape the next chapter in human history.

Creating an environment that is conducive to innovation requires a multifaceted strategy that includes visionary leadership, a creative culture, technical aptitude, international cooperation, ethical concerns, and the ability to overcome obstacles. One thing is clear as we set out on our adventure into the unknown: innovation is a process that never stops and never ends, influencing the direction of human development rather than just a destination.

Chapter 1

Overview of Announcements

Keeping up with the most recent news in the ever-evolving world of innovation and technology is like opening a gateway to the future. Entering this thorough review, we take you on a tour of the ground-breaking discoveries and calculated debuts from the January 2024 Samsung Galaxy Unpacked event. This chapter is our road map, taking us through the major attractions, features that will change the game, and the buzz of excitement that permeated the virtual walls of this virtual extravaganza.

As Samsung opened the curtains to showcase the newest generation of their Galaxy series, the scene was prepared and the crowd was excited. The announcements, which included wearables and smartphones, offered not just a look at the newest technology but also a picture of the technological future that Samsung hopes to create. The main announcements that grabbed attention and established the tone for the rest of the speech are covered in detail in this section.

The Galaxy S24 and Galaxy S24 Ultra, the much awaited replacements for the Galaxy S23 series, were the focal point of the unveiling. A story begins to take shape as we read through the features, specs, and assurances of improved user experiences. This story helps us understand Samsung's vision for the future of smartphones. Each aspect is examined to provide a comprehensive picture of the advancements achieved in the growth of smartphones, from camera advances to the incorporation of artificial intelligence. Surprises are what keep viewers interested in the world of technical unveilings. There were hidden gems and surprising turns hiding among the much-anticipated revelations. This section peels back the layers of the announcements to highlight the details that could have been missed in the initial frenzy, such as a feature that was overlooked or a little design change that might have a big effect.

Samsung's entry into wearable technology is a calculated attempt to include gadgets into our everyday life rather than just as an accessory. This part examines how Samsung is pushing wearable technology limits and showcasing ideas that go beyond the norm, ranging from smartwatches to fitness trackers. The way that practicality, design, and health-related features come together creates a clear image of the wearables market after the Galaxy Unpacked event.

In an environment of technology powered by both software and hardware, announcements about physical gadgets were not limited to that. Samsung's dedication to improving user experiences via software updates was essential to the story's development. This section analyses the software innovations, including redesigned user interfaces, enhanced functionality, and the addition of state-of-the-art capabilities that enhance the user experience in general.

A tantalising peek at the Samsung Ring, an enigmatic item that left viewers guessing and expecting its position in the digital environment, was one of the fascinating revelations. This section explores the teases, rumours, and air of mystery surrounding this latest offering from Samsung, encouraging readers to consider the possible implications of this unannounced gadget.

The statements' formality aside, the tech world came alive with debates, responses, and viewpoints. This section explores the internet conversation, ranging from discussions about camera innovations to discussions about pricing tactics, offering an inside look at the excitement that the Samsung Galaxy Unpacked event created in the community.

This chapter provides the framework for the other inquiries as we immerse ourselves in the summary of announcements. The disclosures, advancements, and community reactions pave the way for a deeper exploration of every aspect, beckoning readers to embark on a voyage across the technical terrain that Samsung will disclose in January 2024.

Unveiling the Latest from Samsung

With innovation being the driving force behind the always changing world of technology, Samsung's most recent reveal is evidence of the brand's dedication to pushing the envelope of what is conceivable. At the Galaxy Unpacked event in January 2024, Samsung unveiled its newest innovations after virtually pulling back the curtains and lighting up the stage with the wonders of modern technology.

Samsung's announcement included the highly anticipated Galaxy S24 and S24 Ultra, both of which are incredible devices in their own right. This section delves into the technical subtleties of these flagship smartphones, analysing the elements that set them apart as the pinnacle of smartphone design. The Galaxy S24 series represents a significant advancement in mobile technology, beyond simple upgrades with its array of advancements, including camera systems that revolutionise mobile photography and AI-driven advances that promise a more intuitive user experience.

Samsung demonstrated state-of-the-art hardware while reaffirming its commitment to improving customer experiences via software upgrades. This section explores the nuances of the software innovations on display during the event. Samsung's software upgrades have a significant impact on the story of easy and intuitive device operation, whether it is via redesigned user interfaces, the addition of new features, or the integration of AI into daily interactions. The Unpacked event showcased more than just smartphones; it also signalled Samsung's entry into wearable technology, an area where technology and daily living coexist together. This section examines how Samsung is changing the wearables market, from smartwatches with advanced health-tracking functions to precisely constructed fitness trackers. Here, the focus is on developments that go beyond the typical and make wearable technology an essential component of our overall well-being rather than merely the anticipated.

Samsung teased us with the mysterious Samsung Ring in the middle of much-anticipated disclosures. This section explores the mystery surrounding this mysterious item, including teases, rumours, and the air of suspense around this surprise addition to Samsung's lineup. What part does Samsung Ring play in the story of Samsung's technology ecosystem as a whole? We investigate the few facts at hand, and our excitement for this unannounced gizmo grows.

The Unpacked event extended beyond the virtual platform, causing a stir in the IT community's discussions, debates, and conversations all across the digital space. This chapter offers an insight into the wide range of thoughts, expectations, and conjectures that surfaced after Samsung's most recent reveal, from social media responses to forum threads breaking down each statement. The excitement in the community attests to the importance and influence of Samsung's technical advancement. It's clear when we peel back the layers of Samsung's most recent reveal that this is a technology voyage rather than just a product demonstration. Samsung's dedication to technological innovation, user-centred design, and smooth integration into our everyday lives paves the way for a time when the lines between the real and virtual worlds will only become thinner. Come along as we examine each aspect in further detail, delving into the nuances and ramifications of Samsung's most recent release.

Chapter 2

Device Highlights

A stunning plethora of gadgets, each serving as a light illuminating the technological future, took centre stage as the Galaxy Unpacked event's curtains fell. This chapter takes us on a tour of the unique characteristics and advancements that set apart the most recent Samsung products, turning them from insignificant trinkets into essential partners in the contemporary digital world.

Samsung's Galaxy S24 series, a technical masterwork that redefines the smartphone experience, is the centrepiece of the company's product lineup. This section examines the key characteristics of the S24 and S24 Ultra, offering a thorough analysis of the improvements that set them apart from their predecessors. The Galaxy S24 series is a testament to Samsung's dedication to pushing the limits of what a smartphone can achieve, from the complexities of camera technology—including ground-breaking improvements in low-light photography and video capabilities—to the integration of artificial intelligence for a more user-friendly user interface.

Samsung unveiled a wearables revolution that transcends the boundaries of smartphones. The most notable aspects of the newest fitness trackers and smartwatches are examined in this chapter. Samsung's wearables are meant to be more than simply accessories—they come with smart devices and smartphone connectivity, as well as sophisticated health monitoring features—and are essential tools for overall well being. The chapter explains the intricate details of performance, design, and creative material application that make these wearables an intriguing addition to the tech world.

Although the Samsung Ring is still a mystery, this chapter explores several theories based on the little details and teases that have been released. We investigate the appeal of this unannounced item by speculating about its uses and features. What function would it serve in the networked world of Samsung's gadgets? How many user interactions and experiences will be revolutionised by it? Even though it was barely audible at Unpacked, the Samsung Ring makes a big impression on us as we examine the world of technology.

Not only were the individual gadgets at Samsung's Unpacked presentation a major feature, but so was the focus on developing a unified software environment. This section walks you through the connecting threads that make Samsung's products work together effortlessly. With features like synchronised experiences and cross-device interoperability, Samsung's software upgrades highlight the company's dedication to providing a comprehensive and connected technology environment. The overall theme emerges when we examine the software highlights: Samsung smartphones are essential parts of a broader, well-balanced ecosystem, not a stand-alone product. The introduction of these gadgets caused a stir not just within the virtual Unpacked event but also on social media, forums, and online groups. The mixture of curiosity, scepticism, and enthusiasm that came out of the tech enthusiasts and people that interacted with the gadget highlights is captured in this part. The community response offers a varied view on how Samsung's current products are received in the wide terrain of tech enthusiasts, ranging from in-depth assessments to real-time replies.

When we go into the standout devices, it's clear that Samsung's technical expertise rests not just in the individual devices but also in the way that hardware, software, and community input are seamlessly integrated. Come along as we examine the subtleties of each gadget, comprehend their role in the greater story of technological advancement, and speculate about how they may affect our digital lifestyles.

- **Decoding the Galaxy S24 Series**

With the release of its much awaited Galaxy S24 series, Samsung has once again taken centre stage in the rapidly changing smartphone market. This chapter explores the complexities of this technological journey, explaining the breakthroughs, improvements, and game-changing elements that characterise the most recent model of Samsung's flagship smartphone series.

Design Elegance:

The elegant design of the Galaxy S24 series, which effortlessly blends form and function, captivates the eye at first look. This section deconstructs the design concept behind these gadgets and examines the fine workmanship, high-quality materials, and ergonomic design elements that enhance their visual attractiveness. Every detail, including the display's curvature and button placement, has been carefully considered to improve the user experience without sacrificing the device's beautiful appearance.

Photography Redefined:

The innovative camera technology of the Galaxy S24 series, which pushes the limits of what smartphones can do in terms of photography and filmmaking, is one of its distinguishing qualities. This section analyses the breakthroughs in cameras, ranging from higher pixel counts to improvements in sensor technology. Explore the realm of computational photography, low-light capabilities, and artificial intelligence integration to comprehend how the Galaxy S24 series is poised to revolutionise mobile photography standards.

AI Integration:

With the Galaxy S24 series, artificial intelligence takes centre stage, making these smartphones into smart friends. Examine the ways that AI improves the user experience in a variety of areas, such as tailored camera settings and app recommendations. This section explores the subtleties of integrating AI, showing how it adjusts to user behaviour, picks up on preferences, and improves the device's overall usefulness.

Beyond the Bezel:
For Samsung, the display has always been the main attraction. With immersive technology that extends beyond the bezel, the Galaxy S24 series carries on this legacy. This chapter examines the latest developments in display technology, such as improved HDR, dynamic AMOLED screens, and faster refresh rates. Recognize how these features enhance the visual experience to a whole new level while using your smartphone for gaming, multimedia consumption, or simple navigation.

The Internal Powerhouse:
The powerful performance of the Galaxy S24 smartphones is hidden under their elegant exteriors. This section walks over the internal parts, showing how Samsung has optimised every element to provide a fluid and responsive user experience, from state-of-the-art CPUs to well-tuned software. The Galaxy S24 series boasts performance that goes above and beyond expectations, whether multitasking, gaming, or running resource-intensive programs.

Network and Beyond:
As the 5G era progresses, connection becomes more important, and the Galaxy S24 series is up to the challenge. This section looks at how various gadgets take use of 5G technology to provide better connection overall, quicker download speeds, and reduced latency. The chapter also discusses various aspects of connection, including enhanced Wi-Fi performance and developments in Bluetooth technology.

Lithium-ion Battery:

A technical wonder would be incomplete if its power source was not long-lasting. Explore the Galaxy S24 series' battery advances, including improvements in rapid charging, efficient power management, and environmentally responsible projects. Recognize how Samsung wants to support people' digital journeys by making sure that their devices are durable and powerful.

Deciphering the Galaxy S24 series reveals that Samsung's most recent flagship smartphones are more than simply minor improvements; rather, they are proof of the company's steadfast dedication to innovation. Come along on this technical journey with us as we explore the many facets of the Galaxy S24 series, including its innovative design, cutting-edge cameras, AI integration, immersive displays, unmatched performance, improved connection, and long-lasting battery solutions.

- **Galaxy Ring Teaser:**

January 18, 2024 Samsung, well-known for its Galaxy Watch line, is pioneering a novel approach by expanding its use to include fingers in addition to wrists. Presenting the Samsung Galaxy Ring, a potentially revolutionary and health-conscious amalgam. Here's what we now know and why it might completely change the wearable technology market.

What to Expect:

Estimated Launch Date: Although a late 2024 launch is anticipated, rumours circulating in the IT community point to an early debut as early as January 2024. Teasers from Samsung's Galaxy Unpacked presentation are adding to the excitement.

Singular Qualities:
With the introduction of a wearable centred on the finger, Samsung has made a significant change with the Galaxy Ring. Though it comes in a much smaller form size, the "powerful and accessible" health gadget is meant to maintain the capabilities of its predecessors.

Insights into Pricing:
Although precise cost information is hard to come by, estimates put it in the ballpark of similar gadgets like the Oura Ring 3.

The Announced Hint:
On January 17, 2024, at Samsung's Galaxy Unpacked event, the formal confirmation was made. The Galaxy Ring, a gadget that has been the subject of rumours since patents were made public in 2022, was on display in the first images. The Samsung Galaxy Ring became official when it was given a trademark by the Korean Intellectual Property Right Information Service (KIPRIS).

The Dilemma of Release:
Setting a release date for this innovative project is difficult. According to The Elec's mid-July estimate, advanced work may result in a 2024 release. Industry sources warn that if medical clearance is required, the schedule may need to be extended, perhaps delaying the release date until 2025.

Features to Look Forward:

Health Monitoring:
The Galaxy Ring is anticipated to have PPG and ECG sensors, replicating features seen in top smart rings and taking cues from patent filings. It may be necessary to monitor temperature and take heart rate readings.

Integration of Smart Homes:
The technological fascination extends beyond health. Integration with a smart home might make it possible to operate linked gadgets like smart TVs, according to a submitted patent.

Sizing Is Important:
There may be only one model with four sizes, according to reports. There are rumours that the first development version is bigger, but features will be trimmed for mass production, and the total size will be less.

Price Tag and Factors:

The world of smart rings is not cheap; it is estimated to cost around $300, similar to that of its rivals. As technology develops, concerns are raised over the use of subscription services, a trend that Samsung's wearable range has not yet followed.

"Is It Better to Wait? A Guide for Thought"

Although the Galaxy Ring is clearly attractive, considering the wearables market's rapid evolution and the uncertainty surrounding its debut, potential customers may choose to consider other options. For those who can't wait, well-known options like the Circular Ring and Oura Ring 3 provide enticing features.

Looking Ahead Galaxy Ring Wishlist:

Expectations are greater, but enthusiasm is higher. Regarding the Samsung Galaxy Ring, we expect:

Advanced Health Metrics:

Detailed health metrics insights that go beyond what the current generation of smart rings can give.

Excellent Sleep monitoring:

The Galaxy Ring is well-positioned to provide precise insights, trends, and coaching without the distraction of a bright screen, thanks to Samsung's advancements in sleep monitoring.

Elegant Design:
To make the Galaxy Ring a subtle but fashionable accessory, a more compact form factor with a variety of colours and finishes is requested.

Still up for debate: will you fall for the Samsung Galaxy Ring craze?

The decision between innovation and the existing options is made as the IT community anxiously awaits.

Chapter 3

Software Updates

The Samsung Galaxy S24 Series Software Updates chapter
covers the evolution of software updates. The Samsung
Galaxy S24 series is proof of the company's dedication to
quality in the rapidly changing field of technology.

- **Firmware Fortification:**

Samsung's quick firmware upgrades demonstrate their
commitment to user security. These upgrades strengthen your
Galaxy S24 against possible hazards by acting as a shield
when threats and vulnerabilities arise in the digital world. The
firmware updates from Samsung keep your device secure,
whether they be security patches, bug fixes, or improved
functionality.

- **Keeping Up with OS Upgrades:**

The Galaxy S24 series develops in the embrace of the most
recent version of Android. Samsung's dedication to delivering
Android upgrades on schedule guarantees that consumers take
advantage of all the enhancements and innovations introduced
by every Android version. The S24 series embraces Android
upgrades and is designed to provide a smooth and modern
user experience.

- **Enhancing User Experience:**

Samsung's One UI, a user interface built for simple navigation and improved functionality, is at the core of the Galaxy S24 series. In Chapter 4, it is discussed how software upgrades serve as a canvas for Samsung to create new user experiences, rather than merely being a means of resolving faults. One UI update transforms how you interact with the device by bringing new features, improvements, and refinements.

- **Rolling Out Features:**

Imagine how your smartphone will change with time, adding new features and capabilities. Samsung makes sure that your Galaxy S24 keeps evolving rather than becoming stagnant. The thrilling voyage of feature rollouts is detailed in Chapter 4; from productivity features to camera improvements, each upgrade opens a new chapter in the Galaxy S24 experience.

- **The Stability Promise:**

Not only do software upgrades guarantee the stability of your device, but they also provide new functions. In Chapter 4, it is explained how Samsung carefully creates upgrades to improve the Galaxy S24 series' overall performance and stability. As the cornerstone, seamless operations provide a dependable and pleasurable user experience.

- **Integrating User Feedback:**

Samsung is dedicated to providing its users with more than just release notes. In Chapter 4, it is examined how user input becomes an essential software update catalyst. Samsung appreciates feedback from users and uses it to customise updates that meet user needs. Your input is important and influences the constant growth of the software landscape for the Galaxy S24.

- **Over-the-Air (OTA) Enchantment:**

The days of laborious updating procedures are long gone. In Chapter 4, the intricacies of Over-the-Air updates are explained, allowing your Galaxy S24 to get the most recent enhancements without interfering with your everyday schedule. These upgrades, which are simple and effective, revolutionise the user experience and guarantee that your gadget is constantly up to date.

Explore the digital world in Chapter 4 as the Samsung Galaxy S24 series changes with every software upgrade. This chapter promises a gadget that changes with you, from feature unveilings to security fortifications. It captures the concept of continual progress. Keep an eye out for the software symphony that Samsung's dedication to innovation and customer happiness has created for your Galaxy S24.

Elevating User Experience through Software

In the intricate dance between hardware and user interaction, the heartbeat of a device is often its software. Chapter 4 of the Samsung Galaxy S24 series intricately explores the realm where technology meets user experience, diving deep into how software innovations elevate the overall interaction with the device.

- **One UI:**

At the core of the Galaxy S24's software experience lies One UI, Samsung's bespoke interface designed for seamless navigation. This section delves into how One UI orchestrates a symphony of harmony, offering an intuitive and user-centric design. From streamlined menus to thoughtful gestures, Samsung's commitment to an interface that understands users shines through.

- **User Personalization:**

No two users are the same, and Chapter 4 unveils how Samsung's software caters to individual preferences. Dive into the world of user personalization, where the Galaxy S24 adapts to your habits and desires. Whether it's customising the home screen, tweaking settings, or choosing themes, this section explores how the device becomes uniquely yours.

- **Fluid Performance:**

A harmonious user experience is incomplete without smooth and responsive performance. This part of the chapter delves into how Samsung's software updates ensure the Galaxy S24 maintains a rhythmic flow. From optimizations to bug fixes, every update contributes to the device's performance, promising a symphony of efficiency in every interaction.

- **Seamless Connectivity:**

In a world where connectivity is key, breaking down digital barriers. Whether it's enhanced Bluetooth capabilities, faster Wi-Fi connections, or improved data transfer protocols, this section delves into how Samsung's software ensures a seamless and connected experience.

- **Intelligent Assistance:**

User experience is not just about what you see but also about how the device anticipates your needs. Discover the role of intelligent assistants in Chapter 4, where Bixby becomes the conductor of convenience. From voice commands to predictive actions, explore how Samsung's software makes your interaction with the Galaxy S24 not just efficient but almost intuitive.

- **Accessibility:**

Samsung's commitment to inclusivity shines through in the software design. This part of the chapter explores how accessibility features are seamlessly integrated, ensuring that every user can participate in the symphony of technology. From voice-guided commands to text-to-speech, Samsung's software strives to make the Galaxy S24 experience accessible to all.

Each line of code contributes to the symphony, ensuring that your interaction with the Galaxy S24 is not just a usage but an experience worth savouring – a symphony of innovation orchestrated to elevate your digital journey.

Chapter 4

Trade-In Programs and Pricing

In the constantly changing world of consumer electronics, trade-in programs have become essential, and Samsung leads the way with an attractive package. This chapter explores the nuances of Samsung's Trade-In program and how its smooth operations, alluring incentives, and dedication to sustainability improve user experience.

The Trade-In program from Samsung makes upgrading a more efficient and cost-effective experience than it would otherwise be. Consumers may exchange their outdated electronics, including as wearables and smartphones, for quick trade-in credits that can be used to the cost of a new Galaxy product. This reduces budgetary obstacles for people looking for the newest advancements and makes upgrades more accessible.

The inclusiveness of Samsung's initiative is what makes it unique. It expands the trade-in offer to a wide variety of gadgets, including tablets, wearables, and even non-Samsung items, rather than just smartphones. This vast range guarantees that the trade-in program serves a broad audience and accommodates users with different tastes.

There are four simple steps in the trade-in process. First, users choose the Galaxy smartphone they want and the matching trade-in device. The trade-in gadget is then prepared by making sure it satisfies eligibility standards. In the third phase, the gadget is sent utilising the packaging from the just purchased Galaxy mobile in an environmentally responsible way. Ultimately, consumers evaluate the trade-in procedure while being reassured that Samsung would return the gadget at no cost to them if their trade-in is rejected, highlighting openness and customer trust.

Samsung's story highlights the company's dedication to sustainability. With an emphasis on reuse, reduction, and recycling, the firm promises to give outdated electronics a new lease of life. In addition to being in line with the rising environmental concerns, this presents Samsung as a conscientious participant in the electronics sector. The Trade-In program is a part of a bigger loyalty scheme and is not limited to single transactions. In addition to receiving immediate savings, users benefit from an eco-friendly strategy that lowers the amount of electronic trash produced. The ideals of today's consumers are in line with this blending of sustainability and economic rewards.

Samsung ensures that customers are aware of the value of their trade-ins and the associated credits by arranging a clear pricing scheme. With price transparency, Samsung's reputation as a company that appreciates its customers more than just a transaction is cemented and trust and loyalty are fostered.

Essentially, the Trade-In program from Samsung makes the process of upgrading a pleasant one. Economic viability, inclusiveness, sustainability, and user delight are all skillfully combined to create a harmonious whole where responsible technology usage and affordability coexist. This chapter tells the story of Samsung's trade-in program as more than just a transaction—rather, it's a life-changing experience that helps create a world where technology is more widely available and electronic waste is reduced.

Navigating the Galaxy Trade-Ins and Pricing Strategy

When it comes to pricing and trade-ins, Samsung takes a calculated strategy that makes things dynamic for consumers looking for the newest Galaxy handsets. The business uses a pricing technique called "price skimming" to maximise profits and market share, especially when introducing cutting-edge and in-demand items.

Trade-In Program for Galaxy

Customers may trade their old smartphones for credits toward a new Galaxy purchase via Samsung's Trade-In Program. In contrast to some rivals, Samsung welcomes a variety of gadgets, including ones that are broken, which helps to adopt a sustainable strategy by repurposing outdated technology.

How It Operates

1. Choose Your Device:
To see quick trade-in credit, choose both your trade-in device and the new Galaxy device you wish.

2.Set Up Your Device: Verify that your device satisfies the eligibility criteria and follow the instructions to reset or disable anti-theft features.

3. Ship Your Device: Encourage waste reduction by sending the trade-in in the box that comes with your new device.
4. **Check & Finish:** Concede with assurance, since Samsung provides a complimentary return of your gadget in the event that it is rejected, subject to certain terms.

Advantages

- **Latest for Less:** Samsung allows consumers to save on their upgrades with attractive trade-in prices.

- **Instant Savings:** There are no upfront costs since the trade-in value is instantly applied during the purchase.

- **Acceptance of damaged Devices:** Setting itself apart from the competition, Samsung's inclusive strategy allows consumers to trade in damaged devices.

Price Skimming as a Pricing Strategy

Setting high pricing at first for new releases in order to draw in early adopters and premium consumers is known as price skimming. Samsung employs this tactic when introducing flagship models such as the Galaxy S and Z series.

Benefits

1. Supply and Demand & ROI: High starting pricing, particularly for innovative items, aid in early investment recovery and improve return on investment.
2. Brand Image: High-end pricing enhances a brand's reputation by attracting customers who see expensive goods and services as exclusive and of superior quality.

3. Market Analysis: By skimming, Samsung is able to examine market categories and get knowledge about the preferences and actions of its customers.

Difficulties

1. Pricing Objectives: Reducing costs after launch might turn off early adopters and damage the product's perceived exclusivity.

2. Relative Competition: Customers may choose competing items if Samsung sets prices too high, thus it is important for the company to take this into account.

Samsung's pricing strategy and Galaxy Trade-In Program are in line with consumer expectations, sustainability objectives, and market circumstances. Samsung successfully navigates the competitive smartphone market by mixing price skimming with trade-in incentives, providing a win-win situation for both the corporation and its consumers.

Chapter 5

Community Reactions

Within the tech world, Samsung's inventive products, pricing policies, and activities often elicit a range of responses. Let's investigate how the public feels about important issues such as Samsung's pricing policy and the Galaxy Trade-In Program.

Trade-In Program for Galaxy

Gratifying Responses:

1. Gratitude for Sustainability: Samsung's acceptance of a wide variety of gadgets for trade-in, even broken ones, has garnered praise from many consumers for their dedication to sustainability. This fits nicely with the expanding consumer demand of ecologically sensitive products.

2. Upgrade Incentive Programs: The community as a whole recognizes the useful advantages of the Trade-In Program, which gives customers an easy method to get the newest Galaxy devices while still getting competitive trade-in prices.

Suggested Improvements:

1. Eligibility Concerns: A few consumers voice their worries over the eligibility requirements, asking Samsung to give more precise instructions to guarantee a more seamless trade-in procedure.

2. Processing Time: Although trade-in credits are applied instantly, there are sporadic comments on the length of time required for trade-in device evaluation and processing.

Price Skimming as a Pricing Strategy

Gratifying Responses:

1. Perceived Value: Fans often see Samsung's price premium as an indication of the superior quality and inventiveness found in its flagship products, which helps to foster a favourable perception of the company.

2. Understanding of Market Dynamics: The technologically astute public recognizes Samsung's strategic cognizance of market dynamics, using price skimming to optimise profits in the wake of new introductions.

Evaluative Viewpoints:

1. Potential Alienation: Some early adopters voice worries about possible price reductions after launch, fearing what would happen to the perceived worth and exclusivity of their original purchase.

2. Competition Dynamics: Community conversations centre on Samsung's need to strike a careful pricing balance in order to remain competitive without alienating consumers to other manufacturers.

The IT community's reactions to Samsung's tactics are a mixture of praise and constructive criticism. Praise is given to the Galaxy Trade-In Program for taking the environment into account, and talks on price skimming dive into the challenges of striking a balance between perceived value and market competitiveness. These responses add to the continuing discussions over Samsung's influence on the development of smartphones.

Echoes from r/samsung: User Sentiments Unveiled

Examining the vibrant Samsung-loving community on Reddit at r/Samsung offers insightful information on the attitudes, conversations, and viewpoints that are shared among members. Let's explore the resonances that exist in this virtual environment.

Accolades and Joy

1. Inventive Items: Customers are always happy to share their admiration and enthusiasm for Samsung's cutting-edge goods, such the newest Galaxy handsets. Modern cameras, innovative display technologies, and special features are often the subject of attention.

2. Adopting a Positive Attitude: Positive experiences with Samsung's software upgrades, warranty assistance, and customer service are often shared by members. These endorsements help to create a favourable brand image in the community.

Remarks and Issues

1. Optimization of Software: Talks usually revolve on Samsung's user interface and software optimization strategy. Some customers voice complaints or provide enhancements on the general responsiveness and performance of Samsung products.

2. Talks About Bloatware: The issue of pre-installed applications, sometimes known as "bloatware," is frequently brought up. Users debate how to control or uninstall these programs and voice their thoughts on their needs.

Trade-In Program for Galaxy

1. Experiences with Trade-In: Individuals often discuss their interactions with the Galaxy Trade-In Program. Positive experiences—where everything goes well and credits are applied without incident—as well as helpful criticism on eligibility requirements and assessment openness are common.

2. Attention to the Environment: The subject of environmental awareness is noteworthy. People who value Samsung's environmental initiatives, particularly the Galaxy Trade-In

program, have conversations about the larger implications for reducing e-waste.

Customization and Requests for New Features

Feature Request List: Users may express their feature suggestions and desired enhancements for next Samsung products via the community. These conversations bring to light the preferences and expectations of users.

2. Customization Talks: Users' desire to personalise their Samsung experience to suit their tastes is evident in discussions about customising their devices with themes, widgets, and customised settings.

User Conversations

1. Aid and Assistance: Members actively assist other users with problem-solving, solution-sharing, and tip-sharing. A climate of support is fostered by the collaborative attitude of the community.

2. Comparing Products: Discussions comparing Samsung products to those of other companies are frequent. When selecting TVs, smartphones, and other Samsung goods, users provide insights into their decision-making processes.

Essentially, r/Samsung becomes a lively community where people debate areas for improvement, applaud Samsung's accomplishments, and actively contribute to forming the overall experience of owning a Samsung device. This community's resonances reveal a varied spectrum of opinions, which makes it a useful resource for fans and those looking to learn more about the Samsung environment.

Chapter 6

Challenges and Concerns

While Unpacked 2024 brought forth a myriad of innovations and promises, it also surfaced several challenges and concerns that warrant attention and strategic navigation:

1. Foldable Technology Adoption: The revolutionary foldable devices showcased at Unpacked 2024 face the challenge of widespread adoption. Consumer readiness, durability concerns, and the need for robust app ecosystems compatible with folding screens pose hurdles to the seamless integration of foldable technology into mainstream usage.

2. AI Ethical Considerations: The pervasive integration of artificial intelligence raises ethical concerns around user privacy, data security, and the potential for bias in AI-driven decision-making. As AI becomes more deeply ingrained in everyday devices, addressing these ethical considerations becomes paramount to fostering trust among users.

3. Interoperability and Ecosystem Integration: Samsung's vision of interconnected living spaces relies on seamless interoperability between devices and ecosystems. The challenge lies in ensuring that different manufacturers adhere to common standards, fostering an environment where diverse devices can communicate and collaborate effectively.

4. Sustainability Implementation: While Unpacked 2024 showcased Samsung's commitment to sustainability, the industry faces the challenge of widespread implementation. Balancing innovation with eco-friendly practices requires concerted efforts across the supply chain, from materials sourcing to end-of-life product disposal.

5. Content Security in Connected Environments: The emphasis on interconnected living spaces and smart home innovations introduces concerns about the security of sensitive data. Safeguarding user information and preventing unauthorised access become critical challenges in realising the full potential of connected technologies.

6. Customization Complexity: While user empowerment through customization is a positive aspect, there's a challenge in striking the right balance. Providing extensive customization options without overwhelming users with complexity requires thoughtful design and intuitive interfaces.

7. Competitive Response: The innovations unveiled at Unpacked 2024 set a high bar for competitors. The challenge for Samsung lies in maintaining its competitive edge amid rapid industry advancements and responding effectively to the strategies and innovations introduced by other tech giants.

8. Global Economic and Regulatory Landscape: External factors such as economic shifts and evolving regulations can impact the adoption and success of new technologies. Navigating the dynamic global landscape requires agility and strategic foresight to address unforeseen challenges.

As Samsung ventures into the future shaped by the revelations of Unpacked 2024, addressing these challenges and concerns will be integral to ensuring the successful integration and sustained impact of the showcased innovations. The tech landscape's ability to tackle these hurdles will play a crucial role in shaping the trajectory of technological advancement in the post-Unpacked 2024 era.

Addressing Community Concerns

The tech world responded to Samsung's daring unveiling of its newest technologies at Unpacked 2024 with a mixture of enthusiasm and trepidation. It becomes necessary for Samsung to respond to community concerns in order to build confidence and guarantee that its innovative technologies are well received. The following important facts came to light as a result of the community's response:

1. Transparency in Pricing: The release of innovative gadgets raises questions over their cost. The community is aware of the value proposition behind the innovations and seeks for price structures that are clear. Samsung has to explain its pricing strategy to consumers in order to match their expectations with the technologies that are being shown and their perceived worth.

2. Dedication to Sustainability: Concern for the environment is the top priority for the community. Consumers are becoming more interested in sustainable activities, such as using energy-efficient appliances and eco-friendly materials. It is important to openly express Samsung's commitment to sustainability, addressing concerns about how production and product lifetime affect the environment.

3.   Security and Privacy of Data: As cutting-edge technologies like AI and IoT are integrated, the community stresses how crucial data security and privacy are. In order to encourage people to embrace linked smart devices, Samsung must reassure them that strong security measures are in place to secure sensitive data.

4. Updates and Support for Software: A common issue within the community is how long device software will be supported. It's critical to communicate clearly about the frequency and length of software upgrades, particularly for flagship items. Samsung has to make it clear that it is committed to provide a smooth and modern user experience.

5. Upgradability and Repairability: Reusable and upgradeable gadgets are supported by the community in an age when technological waste is on the rise. In order to allay customer worries and meet sustainability targets, Samsung should prioritise modularity, component accessibility, and maintenance assistance.

6. Accessibility and Inclusivity: The community pays close attention to inclusion features, making sure that new developments in technology meet the demands of a wide range of users. To appeal to a wide audience, Samsung should emphasise its dedication to accessibility, varied user interfaces, and considerations for people with different abilities.

7. Worldwide Accessibility: For the community, making ideas worldwide accessible is a top goal. Samsung should acknowledge the global character of its user base and provide a plan for worldwide availability in order to allay worries about delayed releases in certain countries.

8. Establish Lines of Communication: A lack of communication often leads to community complaints. An open and cooperative connection may be fostered by creating avenues for feedback, responding to inquiries immediately, and actively participating in the community on websites and social media.

Samsung's post-Unpacked 2024 success will depend not just on its technical capabilities but also on how well it handles and resolves these community issues. In the ever-changing world of consumer technology, Samsung can maintain its reputation as a reliable inventor by acknowledging and reacting to the realities expressed by its consumers.

Chapter 7

Future Expectations

A number of significant expectations and trends are beginning to develop as we traverse the technology environment and consider the future of our globally networked society. Let's take a look at the crystal ball of possibilities that the unwritten chapters hold for us.

1. Artificial Intelligence (AI) Advancements:

- Expect unparalleled progress in AI, with uses ranging from sophisticated problem-solving algorithms to individualised virtual assistants.

- It is anticipated that the introduction of AI into many facets of everyday life, business, and healthcare will redefine innovation and efficiency.

2. 5G Revolution and connection:

- A quantum increase in internet speed and connection is promised by the widespread deployment of 5G technology. There will be a noticeable increase in the capabilities of fields like augmented reality (AR), virtual reality (VR), and the Internet of Things (IoT).

3. Sustainability Takes Center Stage:

- Future product design, production methods, and business practices will all be impacted by a rising commitment to sustainability.

- Eco-friendly decisions will be given priority by both enterprises and consumers, which will accelerate the transition to greener technology and circular economies.

4. Health Tech and Digital Wellness:

- Be prepared for a rise in health-related technology, such as wearables that track vital signs and cutting-edge telemedicine programs.
-
- Patient care, preventative measures, and diagnostics will all continue to be revolutionised by the convergence of technology and healthcare.

5. Virtual and Augmented Realities Revealed:

- AR and VR technology will go beyond entertainment and gaming, finding uses in immersive experiences, education, and professional collaboration.

- Augmented overlays and virtual worlds will completely change how we engage with both digital and real-world material.

6. The Evolution of Cybersecurity:

- The importance of cybersecurity will increase as the globe becomes more interconnected. Leading the way will be innovations in safeguarding digital identities and thwarting cyberattacks.

- There will be an evolution of new guidelines and procedures to protect data integrity and privacy.

7. Space Exploration and Commercialization:

- Governmental and commercial organisations will continue to fund large-scale space exploration programs as the race for space exploration continues.

- There may be increased accessibility to commercial space exploration, creating new opportunities beyond Earth.

8. Education Transformed by Technology:

- Personalised learning, online collaboration, and interactive material will become the standard as technology transforms traditional educational methods.

- Digital platforms' ability to support lifelong learning will be essential for adjusting to a labour market that is changing quickly.

9. Cultural Impact of Technology:

- Art, entertainment, and social standards will all be impacted by the growing nexus between technology and culture.

- The cultural landscape will be shaped by new forms of creative expression that are affected by evolving technology.

10. Ethical Issues and Regulations:

- As technology develops, ethical issues pertaining to artificial intelligence, data privacy, and digital rights will become more important.

- It will be difficult for governments and organisations to develop and modify legislation to guarantee the ethical and responsible use of technology.

The future in this dynamic story is a patchwork of chances and problems. Our joint decisions, inventions, and conscientious maintenance of the technological wonders that continue to reshape our planet will determine the next chapters. We look forward to and reflect on the developing tale of our digital era as we flip the page to the next chapter.

What's Ahead for Unpacked 2024

With tantalising views into the future, the tech industry sits on the cusp of a new era as Unpacked 2024 draws to a close. Inspired by the revelations and advancements made during this historic occasion, here is a reflection on the future.

1. Foldable Futures:

- The development of foldable gadgets grabs attention, inspiring ideas for uses that go beyond smartphones.

- As manufacturers investigate new uses, expect to see a profusion of foldable technology, ranging from tablets to non-traditional form factors.

2. AI-Infused Ecosystems:

- Unpacked 2024 hints to a future in which intelligent, context-aware devices work together effortlessly, setting the standard for AI integration across Samsung's ecosystem.

- As AI becomes more important in predicting and meeting customer demands, expect a more seamless and intuitive user experience.

3. Connected Living Spaces:

- Recently unveiled smart home advancements open the door to integrated living areas where gadgets work together to improve security, convenience, and energy efficiency.

- The ecosystem of smart homes develops beyond individual devices to create surroundings that are holistic and responsive to the preferences of the user.

4. Immersive Experiences:

- The convergence of content production and hardware innovation suggests a future where immersive experiences revolutionise work and enjoyment.

- Technologies related to virtual and augmented reality are probably going to be very important, going beyond their present uses and becoming increasingly integrated into everyday life.

5. Sustainability Imperative:

- Samsung's dedication to sustainability is a symptom of a larger trend in the industry toward environmentally friendly operations.

- Anticipate continued efforts to encourage circular economies, lessen environmental effects, and develop green goods.

6. Redefining Mobile Photography:

- The Unpacked 2024 camera advances set the stage for a new era in mobile photography.

- With their revolutionary features and improved photographic capabilities, future gadgets could push the creative envelope.

7. Security and Privacy Focus:

- As everyday life becomes more digitally connected, privacy and security become more important factors to take into account.

- Advanced security mechanisms may be included into Samsung smartphones in the future to protect user information and digital identities.

8. Health Tech Innovations:

- Unpacked suggests that future gadgets would actively improve users' well-being, hinting at a developing relationship between technology and health.

- Fitness tracking, health monitoring, and cutting-edge apps might all become essential components of Samsung's ecosystem.

9. Worldwide Collaboration Initiatives:

- Unpacked 2024 highlights Samsung's alliances and partnerships with worldwide innovators and leaders in the industry, suggesting a trend in this direction.

- Anticipate an increase in cooperative endeavours that challenge the limits of creativity, promoting a varied and ever-changing technology environment.

10. Ongoing User-Centric Approach:

- Samsung's steadfast dedication to user-centric functionality and design is probably going to continue, impacting the creation of new products.

- One of Samsung's primary strategies may continue to be its focus on user customisation and easy interfaces.

The story develops with excitement and promise as we go beyond Unpacked 2024 into the future. Wonders of technology, formed by human demands and ingenuity, are waiting to be discovered beyond the realm of possibility. The voyage ahead seems to be an engrossing investigation of the limitless horizons that appear when creativity and state-of-the-art technology collide.

Conclusion

The technology world has changed dramatically in the wake of Unpacked 2024, exposing a tapestry of advancements that will influence the future. Samsung has ushered in a vibrant era of linked possibilities with the launch of innovative gadgets and strategic initiatives. As we consider the main ideas and conclusions from this historic event, a few conclusions emerge:

Convergence of Intelligence: Unpacked 2024 is a turning point in the way artificial intelligence and daily life are merging. Samsung's dedication to artificial intelligence (AI)-powered ecosystems portends a day when gadgets would effortlessly adjust to user preferences, revolutionising how we engage with technology.

2. Horizons That Fold: The development of foldable electronics is a shining example of innovation, leading to a world where practicality and adaptability coexist. Beyond smartphones, the possibility of foldable technology in a variety of form factors suggests a revolution in personal electronics.

3. Well-Being Environments: A new age of linked living spaces is heralded by the smart home technology on display. Beyond individual devices, Samsung sees a cohesive environment where gadgets work together to improve security, convenience, and energy efficiency.

4. Immersive Experiences Redefined: Unpacked 2024 suggests a future in which work and enjoyment are redefined via immersive experiences. The convergence of content production and hardware innovation suggests a future in which technology plays a central role in defining experiences.

5. Using sustainability as a compass: Samsung's focus on sustainability is indicative of a larger movement in the business toward ethical behaviour. The need to develop technology that respects the environment is in line with the dedication to minimising environmental effect and promoting circular economies.

6. Innovation Focused on Users: Samsung's steadfast dedication to user-centric design is a recurring theme throughout Unpacked 2024. The emphasis on personalization, easy-to-use interfaces, and accommodating changing user requirements highlights a commitment to improving the human experience.

The sounds of invention resound as we make our way across the environment that emerges after Unpacked 2024, pointing to a time when technology will be seamlessly woven into our daily lives. Samsung is paving the way for an exciting new chapter in the history of technology with its efforts toward intelligent, user-friendly, and sustainable solutions. The road ahead is full of opportunities for learning, teamwork, and a never-ending quest for greatness. Unpacked 2024 is more than simply a one-time event—it's a sneak peek into a world where innovation and creativity coexist and limitless opportunities await.
Learnings and Symbols

The Impact of Unpacked 2024

Unpacked 2024 has had a lasting impact on the state of technology by launching a flurry of inventions that might fundamentally alter how we engage with the digital world. Several important lessons and impacts emerge as the business is still feeling the effects of this historic event:

1. Foldable Revolution: A new age in consumer electronics is being ushered in with the introduction of state-of-the-art foldable gadgets. Samsung's dedication to foldable technology not only changes the way we think about smartphones, but it also creates previously unimaginable opportunities for a variety of other device categories. This foldable revolution has the potential to completely change how people interact with and carry about their digital experiences.

2. AI Integration at the Core: Unpacked 2024 highlights how deeply Samsung has incorporated artificial intelligence into its entire line of products. Artificial Intelligence (AI) is a key component in improving the functioning and customization of gadgets, from intelligent assistants to adaptable user interfaces. AI's widespread effect is expected to improve user experiences by increasing the responsiveness and intuitiveness of technology.

3. Interconnected Living Areas: The shown advances in smart homes go beyond standalone devices, exhibiting a completely networked living environment. IoT and smart home ecosystems will provide seamless device interaction, which should improve convenience, energy efficiency, and security. The effects of this integrated strategy are probably going to completely change how people see and interact with their homes.

4. Sustainability as a Driving Force: Unpacked 2024 highlights a paradigm change in the ICT sector toward sustainability. Samsung's dedication to sustainable development, circular economies, and less environmental impact is indicative of a rising understanding of the need for responsible innovation. This strategy, which is motivated by sustainability, has an influence not just on individual items but also on industry procedures and customer expectations.

5. The Intense Content Environment: Users should expect immersive experiences as sophisticated technology and a strong content ecosystem come together to take centre stage. Regardless of the device, Unpacked 2024 establishes the groundwork for a future in which content consumption becomes more compelling due to improvements in audio capabilities and high-quality screens. This change has an influence on users' interactions with information, education, and communication that goes beyond amusement.

6. Customization Promotes User Empowerment: Samsung's focus on customisation and user-centric design allows people to personalise their digital experiences. With features like adaptable features and customised interfaces, Unpacked 2024 demonstrates a dedication to empowering consumers. This user-centric strategy is expected to appeal with customers looking for individualised, user-friendly technologies and strengthen brand loyalty.

Unpacked 2024 is a monument to Samsung's vision of a connected, intelligent, and sustainable future as its effects continue to reverberate across the tech industry. These important lessons learned and factors are likely to have a significant effect much beyond the gadgets on display, impacting consumer expectations, market trends, and the fundamentals of our digital interactions. Unpacked 2024 is a compass that points to a future in which innovation effortlessly synchronises with the changing requirements and desires of consumers.